APPLE WATCH SERIES 5 USER'S GUIDE

THE BEGINNER AND PRO'S ULTIMATE GUIDE TO MASTER YOUR APPLE WATCH SERIES 5 AND WATCHOS 6, COMPLETE MANUAL TO LEARN ADVANCED TIPS AND TRICKS

WENDY HILLS

You are welcome to join the Fan's Corner, here

The Beginner and Pro's Ultimate to Master Your Apple Watch
Series 5 and WatchOS 6, Complete Guide to Learn Advanced Tips
and Tricks

Wendy Hills

Disclaimer

The advice and strategies found within may not be suitable for
every situation. This work is sold with the understanding that
neither the author nor the publisher is held responsible for the
results accrued from the advice in this book.

Apple Watch Series 5 Complete User's Guide

The Beginner and Pro's Ultimate to Master Your Apple Watch Series 5 and WatchOS 6, Complete Guide to Learn Advanced Tips and Tricks

Wendy Hills

Introduction

The Apple Watch may be one of the most important accessories to have for your iPhone, yet on its own, it's also a powerful device and very useful for workouts cataloging, heart rate monitoring, paying for items, playing songs, and, obviously for telling what time it is.

The Apple Watch is specifically designed by Apple as a smartwatch to complement the iPhone, especially when you consider the number of new functions introduced by its manufacturers. The Apple Watch is designed, developed, promoted and sold by Apple Inc. The watch has proven to be a watch that provides a delightful experience to all its users from its earliest versions to every other upgrade with newer versions getting better with the addition of more awesome features and functions to make old users happy and new users wowed. With the world gradually moving into one driven by artificial intelligence, the Apple Watch provides a perfect example of what the future holds in terms of the impact of future technology in our daily lives.

Since the official first launched of the pioneer Apple Watch in April of 2015, the watch has since grown to become one of the most sort-after smartwatches in the world. By the second quarter of that year, Apple had sold more than 4million units of the first version of the Apple Smartwatch. The unexpected success of that initial Apple watch had made it become a luxury to afford since then leading to many other versions or series as they are popularly called to be developed by Apple. This has led to the smartwatch to evolve from being just a fashionable timepiece to become the mind-blowing smartwatch that it has now become with new features introduced in each upgrade.

The longer you use your Apple Watch, the more you may see yourself desiring to get more out of it by accessorizing your iPhone accessory with new bands, coverings for extra protection, external displays, holders, traveling cases and even headphones.

Beyond being a watch to just determine what time of the day it is, it also provides an innovative way of communicating from your wrist combined with its amazing health and fitness features, which makes the Apple smartwatch stand tall amongst its competitors and contributes to it being an enviable watch compared to other smartwatches.

In the Apple announcement in September of 2019, Apple unveiled its latest version (as at the time of writing this book), the Apple Watch Series 5 which comes with the latest WatchOS 6 and a whole lot of exciting new features to keep you engaged.

As expected, many of the guides that come with these devices tend to be at best basic and do not really offer as much help as you would want which is why this guide has been designed to work you through on the best way to get started with your Apple Watch Series 5.

It is also designed to explain how to get the best out of your Apple Watch Series 5 in a simple and easy to understand language.

Chapter One

Introducing the Apple Watch Series 5

As with Apple's previous versions of Apple Watches, the upgraded Apple Watch Series 5 comes with very many features that makes it a standout watch, which is not unexpected when you consider that it was released at the same time as the iPhone 11 pro.

The Apple Watch and iPhone can best be described as two sides of the same coin even though they are two pieces of hardware devices that are distinctly different and need each other to exist. When you start using a new Apple Watch, your first step will be to turn it on, after which you will need to pair it with an iPhone.

To pair your Apple Watch with your iPhone, you'll have to utilize the Watch app on the Apple iOS which will most likely come pre-installed on your iPhone. You can also have it downloaded from the App Store if you've previously removed it.

Just like the series 4, the packaging of the latest series 5 has a similar look. So even though you may find the series 5 similar to the i-watch series 4 packaging, do not be deceived into thinking that they are exactly the same, the i-watch series 5 comes with a new wide range of functions that the i-watch series 4 can only be envious of.

Unboxing of Series 5

As soon as you open the box, you will be able to see the content of the box which includes the watch itself and a couple of other accessories including the charger and the smartwatch's bands.

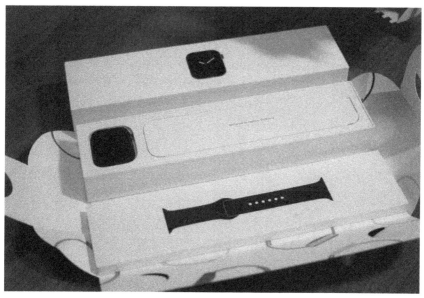

The unboxing process is pretty straight forward even for first time buyers or users. To open the box, all you have to do is to simply unclip the flaps pinned down by dragging them towards either end of the watch's pack and then stretching the extended flap to complete the pack opening process. The watch pack usually comes in varying designs to enable potential buyers of the watch to choose from a list of available colors that best suits their taste.

Once opened, the items you would find in the pack will include the watch itself, its two bands which will come in different sizes (long and short, depending on wrist size of users), the watch charger, and a quick start user guide to assist you in quickly setting up the watch for immediate use. Each included item in the pack is aimed at ensuring a good user experience and customer satisfaction.

Sizes and Pricing

It is important to know that the watch comes with a smaller aluminum 40-millimeter model and the larger 44-mm design. The 40-millimeter model comes with a GPS-only model that goes for $399, whereas the LTE connected model goes for at least $499. However, if you want the ceramic, stainless steel, or titanium model, you can expect the pricing to go up because you will a variety of options to choose from. For the Series 5 edition with the new titanium finish, that starts at $799 whereas the white ceramic comes in at $1,299. For those who are previously used to the gray ceramic in previous versions, that did not return in this new release.

The stainless-steel of the series 5 model seems to favor those who desire a watch that feels and looks a bit high-end compared to the regular aluminum. In the same way, the white ceramic special edition is a great option for those who want a more classic type of watch.

The watchband is designed to be easy to change to any wrist band color and the leather material option of your choices. This means you do not only get a feeling of using a luxury watch but enjoy the privilege of also using the semblance of a customized band-type to make your apple watch series 5 have a special feel.

The watch and its band that you find in the packaging are detachable where you are free to assemble or couple the watch depending on your selected band-type or length. The side of the band that has a hook-like side is slotted into the hollow space designed for attaching the bands. If fixed properly, a sound of a tap in will be heard that indicates that the band has been successfully fixed to the watch itself. The second band is fixed in the same way.

However, if you want to detach the band from the watch, you can use the button on the surface of the watch close to the band slot by tapping it to get the band unhooked and removed by sliding out in the same direction it was slid into it.

Basic Set-Up of the I-Watch Series 5

To set the watch up for use, the power button is tapped for a few seconds, which then powers on the watch. To locate the power button, look for the side button below the button that has the look of the control of a regular wristwatch, which Apple prefers to call Digital Crown.

Easy to Install or Remove

Precise and secure for Apple Watch

When the watch is powered on, the first display you will notice on the watch will be a white apple logo with a black background. Immediately after this will be a pop-up notification requesting you to select a language of choice that the phone will use in displaying its contents. The next option will be the opportunity to pair your iPhone with the apple series 5 watch.

To perform this, go to the control center on your iPhone by swiping up on the main or home screen. Ensure your Wi-Fi and Bluetooth connections are turned on, after which you can go to the apple watch app on your phone and click on Start the pairing. You will immediately be greeted with a screen that displays a command requesting you to place your iPhone beside the watch for pairing. This pairing process will only work for iPhones that run an IOS 8.2 and higher.

Once the applicable iPhone is put beside the Apple watch, a notification will pop up stating that "put on your Apple watch and hold it up to the camera", the pairing process will try to start by displaying a "ball-like connection" on the watch's screen indicating that it is waiting to be paired.

If you have not yet mastered how to use your iPhone camera, especially if you are using the iPhone 11 or iPhone 11 Pro and Pro Max, you may want to also read Mastering the iPhone 11 Pro and

Pro Max Camera and Mastering the iPhone 11 Camera, both by James Nino.

You have to ensure you have the apple watch application installed on your iPhone. If your phone already has the latest IOS update, then you can expect the Watch App to be automatically installed. If, however, you don't have the app installed on your phone, you can do that by simply going to "settings" on your iPhone, click on "General", click on "software update" and make sure it's updated, and if not, you can simply click on "download and install". It might take some time to complete.

When in the process of pairing, you should be mindful of obstructions in the form of plastic film on the watch's screen and phone camera that can hinder the pairing process so as to enhance the ability for both devices to recognize each other and pair easily.

The pairing process is ideally very fast and ordinarily should be completed in less than one minute, after which, the phone screen will display a notification indicating the successful pairing process.

The next setting option on your phone will be to choose on which wrist you plan to wear the apple watch, either left or right depending on your preference and if you are right or left-handed.

Depending on the choices you make in your settings, the phone will calibrate the watch accordingly.

The subsequent messages displayed on the phone's screen will be about providing various guides on how to use the device, as well as Apple's terms and conditions of device use that you will have to agree with in order to continue with the process by clicking the "agree to" button.

After this, you will be requested to enter your "APPLE USER-ID PASSWORD". Once this is done, you will be given the option to turn-on "location services", which can be done by clicking OK, after that you will be requested to activate "SIRI" by clicking OK once again, and then Diagnostics.

However, it is advisable here to choose "Automatically Send" and after which save the selected option by clicking OK.

You can also set the password of the apple watch from the iPhone screen. To do this, you'll be required to create a password from the iPhone which you can easily do by typing your selected secret characters known only to you as your security password.

The second set-up aspect involves pairing the iPhone with the watch's cellular service. And this will simply pop-up as a notification on the phone after the first set up, indicating that the cellular set-up can be activated depending on your watch's model. This is necessary so that when the watch is in use, it can be made to work like a phone that you can use it even when the phone is not within range.

To activate this function, you will need to select the pop-up notification stating, "Cellular Set-up" and click on "Set-up cellular", This option is usually found after the phone has displayed a number of permission notifications that include but not limited to; Enable Route Tracking, Shared settings, and Create a password.

The iPhone will display further notification settings, especially for feature display. Depending on your preference, some notifications can be accepted or skipped.

At the end of the notification settings following the above-listed steps, the watch will begin a full synching process that can last from anything between ten to fifteen minutes before the watch is fully synced.

During this synching process, the watch will display a notification "Apple Watch Basics" showing a loading circle indicating the level of progress, as well as the present time.

After the watch has completed the syncing process, it'll display a notification that your Watch Is Ready, along with the "Ok sign". Press the Digital Crown to start.

With that out of the way, the phone will now be ready for full use.

Basics of Apple Watch Series 5

Digital Crown/
Home button

Side button

Powering

To turn on the apple watch, you simply press and hold the side button for a few seconds. Immediately after doing this, you'll see the Apple logo display on the watch screen. Similarly, to power off the apple watch, you press and hold the side button, then slide to the right the displayed power off icon.

Turning on Sleep Mode

When the Apple Watch is in sleep mode, you can activate it by bringing the watch close to your face or by simply tapping the screen to activate the watch for display and or activity. Similarly, you can put the watch back to sleep mode by dropping your wrist away from your face which has the effect of triggering the phone into sleep or inactive mode.

Using the Apple Watch Digital Crown

At first glance it will seem that it has the looks of the knob of a regular watch however on further investigation you will find that it has more advanced functions than the regular watch knob that often only has a primary function of setting Date and time on regular watches. The digital crown, on the other hand, can be used for an array of functions like Zoom and scrolling through the watch.

In addition to the digital crown on the watch, there is a home button which acts as the regular home button on the iPhone.

To use the home button, you simply click on the flat surface beside the digital crown which will open up the main display page of the watch on the next display showing all available apps or icons on display, ready for use.

By pressing the same home page, the display goes back into the default clock display background. This, in summary, shows that a single tap of the home button will take you to the home page from the default clock display to the home page where all apps or icons are displayed and ready for use.

Also, the display button can take you back to the home page from any of the apps that are in use by minimizing the current activity on the home page which you wish to quit completely.

By double-tapping the home button which is the flat surface of the watch, you will be taken to the previous page in use. This is useful when you minimize an app or apps in use. By performing the same double tapping action again, your display goes back to the app prior to that. By tapping and holding, the feature "Siri" is activated.

Side Button

The side button on the Apple Watch Series 5 performs a lot of functions, some of which include displaying of frequently dialed contact. So, you can simply scroll through them using the digital crown and select any contact you wish to select by clicking on the desired contact on the screen.

Once a contact has been selected, a number of other operations can be performed on it through the displayed options which include sending messages, voice calls, heartbeat and sending pictures to other users who also have the apple watch series.

Also, by double-tapping the side button, you can activate the "Apple Pay" feature on the watch.

Equally, pressing and holding the side button will display the menu/icons, that allow you to power on or off the watch.

Some of the components of the apple watch series-5 also include the speaker located under the watch's face, which also happens to be directly opposite the digital crown, a micro-phone which is also in the same location as the speaker, and a heart rate monitor sensor which is to monitor your heart rate while you're doing your exercises.

Charging Port

The apple watch has a unique charging port. Unlike regular charging ports that have slots in spaces which, when extended can slot in projected metal chips, the apple watch, on the other hand, has a unique magnetic charging surface that is affixed to the watch underneath. The other end of the magnetic surface which is connected by a regular apple cord is where the charging adapter is, customarily connected to a power source or socket, or even USB slot in cases where a USB power source is used instead.

When you have finished charging the watch, the charger can easily be disconnected by detaching the magnetic strip from the watch's back.

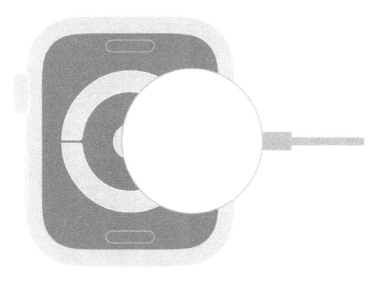

Chapter Two

Detailed Review of Apple Watch Series 5

The makers of the Apple Watch Series have once again shown in the new series 5 that they are not contented with the successes they achieved with the previous Apple series watches. The Apple Watch Series 4 was a wonderful masterpiece of tech design and being a relatively new product in the tech world, it had its first version released in 2005, the Series 4 which was the last series before the Series 5 portrayed great improvement and advancement within the short time frame.

Apple aims to dominate the smartwatch market with the constant introduction of innovative features and tech designs to unleash and produce the now excellent Apple Watch Series 5. Apple has demonstrated its intention to produce a consistent and quality product with great impressive health features with its new Apple Watch Series 5.

The Series 4 of the Apple Watch came with a unique ECG feature that enabled the watch to detect signs of atrial fibrillation. ECG measures the electrical activity of the heart, providing vital information such as heart rate, heart rhythm, etc. This made the Series 4 Watch to be touted as a life-saving device. The series 4 even made it possible for you to change the dimensions and shape of the smartwatch as well.

The new Apple Watch Series 5 is not significantly different from series 4. However, one unique upgrade of the previous series 4 version is the "always-on display" feature. Unlike before where you had to move your wrist to check your watch, on the series 5 you no longer need to flick your wrist to check the time and any notification that pops up from time to time. And with this unique feature, it becomes similar to an actual watch. The Apple Watch Series 5, with the improved new screen design, prevents the battery from easily being drained. It also comes with an inbuilt compass.

Also, the WatchOS 6 update that comes with the new series has a lot of new interesting features that make it smarter than previous versions. The Series 5 Apple Watch has some subtle improvements which makes it a watch that provides luxury.

The Design

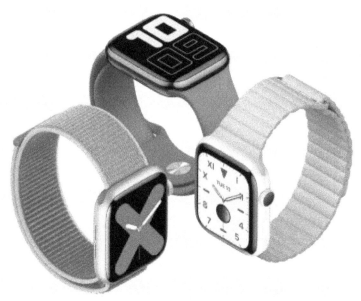

Similar to the series 4, the Apple watch series 5 comes in sizes 40mm and 44mm with no major distinction in the overall difference in over-all design. It is almost similar to that of series 4.

However, there is a difference in the new arrangement of materials and colors to select from. This includes the new titanium finish that is brushed, and it comes in either black or gray color. It has a weight that is around 36 grams when compared to the stainless steel, even though it cost about $100 more than the stainless steel. One can barely notice the watch on your wrist, and it is almost impossible to get your shirt cuff, stuck under. The curvy case, which is still a svelte 10.7mm, makes it a wonderful design for comfort and efficiency.

Another design that is replicated in the Series 5 Apple Watch is the ceramic model that costs as much as $1,299. The cheapest in the series 5 is the GPS-only in aluminum, which costs around $399. Each model offers options for GPS-only or cellular. The Cellular cost more from $499 upwards.

In addition to the ceramic and titanium options, the watch comes with leather bands and also a Milanese gold loop. With the new change in the purchase process both online and in stores, one can purchase any band you want to match your Apple Watch. Customizing your Watch becomes much better and easier as Apple's partnerships with Nike and Hermès, offering custom-fit bands and watch faces.

The Always-On Watch Display

The most striking, unique feature of the Apple Watch Series 5 that was not in previous versions, is the always-on screen. This is made possible as a result of the new Low-Temperature Polycrystalline Oxide display known as the LTPO. This wonderful feature helps to reduce the refresh rate, thereby preventing the screen from consuming much power. This feature becomes activated when you put your wrist down by the side or cover the screen with a hand. The display becomes dim and some animations like the second-hand stop. According to Apple, this reduces the refresh rate, from 60Hz to as low as 1Hz.

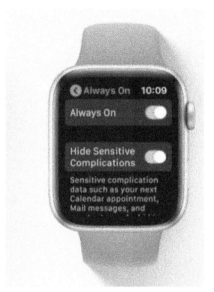

This is a huge change for the series 5 compared to the series 4 Apple Watch. The feature enables you to view the time in real-time as a regular watch would.

With this unique feature, you can do your workouts and at the same time, check the watch to see your data without having to stop. Workouts details can be displayed on the run as a result of the "Always on Display" feature which makes it more user–friendly. This was impossible with the previous Apple Watch Series. Some of Apple's apps have been redeveloped to enable this feature also. Apps that are not designed to do anything with the always-on screen display, including third-party apps, will blur what is on display, while the digital clock appears as an overlay.

While this feature might not seem like a big deal to some, it makes the Apple Watch Series 5 look more like a regular watch and less like a computer. One can actually view the time by merely taking a glance at it, which seems to be one of the most annoying aspects of having to turn on the screen on the previous Apple Watch Series.

The WatchOS 6 Features

Apart from the "Always on Display" feature which seems to be a novel development of Series 5, this new apple watch also comes with an updated operating system called the WatchOS 6. This new OS has a lot of innovative apps and is available for updates in other series with the exception of the first release of the Apple Watch. It comes with some interesting new additions such as the gentle tap you get on your wrist at the hour mark compared to the archaic "beep beep" sound you get hourly in many digital watches.

The compatibility of the Apple Watch and WatchOS 6 is quite amazing and in terms of excellent performance and its ease of use and user experience, the Apple Watch Series 5 beats all its rivals, hands down. Aside from it being fun to use, the haptic feedback gives you a confident feeling and a sense of touch against your wrist or finger. It also gives you an awesome feeling zooming in and out of the app screen using the Digital Crown. This indeed is a masterpiece that shows cohesiveness and smartness.

It is quite easy to set up the process with no hassles whatsoever. It takes around 10 minutes to finish the setup from the first time the watch is turned on to when it is paired with the iPhone. The pairing process is also seamless and easy.

There is a dedicated App Store on the Apple Watch Series 5 which is another remarkable feature. You do not need to first download apps on your iPhone and then sync them to your watch, especially for certain apps. All you need to do is to go to the Home Screen and search either by dictation or scribbling and a list of popular apps would be displayed, from which you can scroll through to download anyone of your choice.

The on-watch App Store that is being included in the upgrade is another move to make the watch as independent as possible from the iPhone. Once a connection either with a phone or directly over a cellular is established, you are now ready to download apps directly to the Apple Watch. Whether this move is a welcome development or not, is another debate on its own. It is believed that many developers would respond to the demand created by this change to create Watch apps that can run without the aid of an iPhone. However, some users still prefer to browse over a phone than a tiny Watch screen.

Also worthy of note too are the addition of new apps, are, calculator, Audiobooks app and different health apps.

Next on the upgraded software review of the Apple watch series 5 is the touch of the uniqueness of Siri, which is merged with Apple-owned Shazam. It enables you to ask it various questions like what song, is being played so that you can add it to your playlist. You can instruct Siri to assist in searching for topics and then scroll through the web results that are displayed on your Apple Watch.

The compass feature, however, is restricted to the Series 5 models. Just like a normal compass, the compass app takes elevation and inclined measurements. The compass has a relatively high level of accuracy even though it is possible for some magnetic bands to alter the accuracy of the compass.

This new WatchOS 6 comes with some issues which are not really much of a problem. When the Watch faces hibernation over a notification under view or any app like the new compass, the background becomes dim while the time is shown at the top right corner making it unattractive to some people. To perform a task, you need to wake the watch up. It would require you to pause for a second before you can interact with the screen when you tap the display. This is the only time the software appears to be slow.

This is a great app for people who go hiking. But the downside to its functionality, especially relying on it for directions when lost in the wild, is that it requires charging daily as the smartwatch obviously cannot run more than a day without charging.

If using a compass to find your way out when lost in some adventure does not help, the improved Series 5's SOS function should bail you out. This feature enables you to make calls to emergency services in any country you are located in. You will be connected with the appropriate first responder. This is only possible for those who have the cellular version.

Another interesting new feature is Apple's Noise app. This app observes and keeps track of sound around you. It notifies you when you are in a loud environment or exposed to noise levels that could impair your hearing.

The app has the capacity to measure around 74 decibels and will give you a warning when the sound level reaches 100 decibels. This feature introduced in the new Apple Watch Series buttresses

Apple's consistent commitment to health, which provides an extra level of environmental awareness.

Interestingly, there is a new tab that can be found on the Activity app on your iPhone known as Trends. It provides a detailed analysis of your activity and information about your overall fitness over 90 days in comparison to the last 365 days. The WatchOS 6 has a Menstrual Cycle Tracking app that can predict both your period and fertility window. It enables a female user to enter their information about their cycles, which gives a breakdown in the iPhone Health app for you to view.

The Battery Life Performance

With the unique "Always on Display" mode being turned on, the longevity of the Series 5 Apple Watch battery life is being reduced just by a small percent. According to Apple's claim, that, the Apple Watch should last approximately the same amount of time when you turn off the "Always on Display" mode. The battery can still go for a full day when used moderately and can be stretched to a day and a half with low usage. The Series 5 comes with new features that add extra pressure on the battery. This hinders the new model's capacity to stretch the battery out up to two days of regular usage. The battery life will reduce with the frequent use of the call features in a cellular Apple Watch. Also, a prolonged period of fitness tracking using the GPS and heart rate monitoring would further strain the battery even then, it is still able to last for a full day's use.

Previous Series of the Apple Watch suffer a lag in the required level of performance of which the Series 5 never suffers except when strained using apps that require data. The performance of the Series 5 is however fast and smooth. The chip inside the Series 5 adds no much performance gain, but instead focuses more on efficiency.

The Watch hardly crashes or freezes on usage. It has an upgraded 32GB, enabling people to download music and podcasts they can listen to or watch as they exercise. This is a welcome feature for those who would love to exercise without a phone and see no need to go for the cellular model.

The Apple Watch Series 5, arguably, remains the best smartwatch for iPhone. The new remarkable "Always on Display" feature and the inclusion of a compass are a welcome development, even though not everyone seems to see the need for those features. The best new features of the Series 5 Apple Watch come with the WatchOS 6. Some of these features can also work on the older series.

The Apple series 5 watch keeps a comprehensive picture of your wellbeing as it builds up a database of information about your health over time, which makes the watch an outstanding device compared to other watch brands. It is able to include supplementary tracking which has the capacity to be the difference between life and death in certain situations. It is able to keep track of your net calorie intake, number of steps taken within a period, hourly movement, relaxation, time spent standing and also tracks all your workouts, including biking, jogging, hiking, swimming, and even activities like yoga. As more information gets collated, it begins to draw up a trend, which can then be used to help you to make correct lifestyle decisions and make any required change that can help improve the state of your health.

Warranty

Lastly, the Apple Watch Series 5 has a one-year warranty that covers manufacturing defects. AppleCare+ is also offered for more comprehensive cover for a fee of about $50 for two years.

The Apple Series 5 is a good buy at the moment and competes better when compared with other smartwatches in terms of convenience, performance, sleekness, or fitness tracking.

Chapter Three

Features and Configurations of The Apple Watch Series 5

There are a considerable number of features the Apple series 5 Watch has that are unique and exclusive to it. Prominent among these features is the Meridian face with its multi-themes that fades away (from white to dark color) when you are not looking at the watch's face.

Having a variety of watch display faces and designs when using its inbuilt feature for modifying and customizing the display faces is one of the upgrades that users of the new Apple Watch Series 5 can enjoy.

So, for those who wish to try out other styles different from the default theme style of this particular watch design, you have the option to edit or modify any of the existing ones to how you want it by touching the center of the watch's screen. The watch will then go on to display an icon on the screen stating "Customize" to give you the ability to change your theme color, display other background colors like purple, orange, red, pink, and black among other colors.

Switching the colors is easy, it can easily be done by using the rotating key located on the side of the watch. You can also use the key when changing other important watch features like date, UV index, voice memos, walkie-talkie, etc.

The "California" watch face is another watch face design style available on the Apple Watch Series 5. It has a cool blue default color. Just like the Meridian display, the California display type can be also be changed easily including its background color, number styles and alphabets.

You also have the option to change the displayed screen size by reducing it from a full to a reduced size, circular or square displays. The Apple Watch Series 5 also allows you to easily add frequently used applications on the home page in order to allow for quick and easy access.

Similar to the Meridian display and California display is another display theme type called the Numerals duo. This is a nice and simple block design that has just the date and time display. The displayed styles and colors are also available to be customized. You can try out the different faces to see the one that works best for you.

The mergular compact is another type of screen display on the apple watch series 5. This spectacular screen display comprises of the clock display, weather report, as well as current Geo-location. It can also be customized in different styles and formats like analog display format, digital format, color styles, set reminders, screen combinations, and complications.

One other feature that has been included in the Apple Watch Series 5 has been the addition of a calculator app. This calculator app is able to perform basic arithmetic calculations as well as some advanced levels of calculations that include percentage, ratio, and squares. To access this advanced feature, you only need to click on the word "Tip" displayed on the watch's screen.

For those who like to do basic calculations on the go, they can easily add the calculator to the watch's main display face for you to perform all your calculations on the go. As usual, to return home on the phone you have to tap the digital crown to go back to the home display.

Another cool upgrade on the Apple watch series 5 is that you are now able to view the Safari browser directly from the watch's screen, and no longer need to depend on your iPhone alone like in the previous series. This is particularly useful for people who want to access "Siri", which when requested can offer to open the search results page to be explored on an individual level.

An additional feature to the watch 5 series upgrade is the voice recording app that allows you to make voice memos directly from your apple watch. All you have to do is to tap the voice record button to record voice memos and click stop when you are through with the recordings, which can be shared or deleted based on your preference.

The gradient apple watch face is another remarkable feature of the device, which when the hand changes, the displayed gradient on the watch is changed, giving it an artistic and fun-like appearance.

Clicking on it will give an array of customizing options, especially displayed color. The displayed design here as well can either be full screen or circular. The full screen does not support the addition of applications on display, but with the circular screen, this can be achieved.

As already stated, one other useful app added to the apple watch series 5 is the noise app. This app allows you to measure the sound levels in decibels present in a surrounding environment and raises an alarm when the noise level is no longer safe for you which in effect will help to protect you from the hazardous effect of a noisy environment capable of damaging your hearing.

The Solar Guide

The Solar Guide works by changing the way the clock is displayed on the screen around the watch's face as the day goes on. The display as well can be customized by clicking the customize button, which then offers you a lot of modifying features that include, but not limited to the selection of an analog time to digital time and complications around the face of the watch.

Notwithstanding the customized style selected by you, the elegant look of the apple series 5 watch is expected to be guaranteed.

An App That Can Earn You Money on The Apple Series 5

By completing a simple survey on an app called Quick Thoughts Earn rewards, you can easily get access to a number of cash rewards on the apple watch series 5.

To get started, open Safari web browser on your connected iPhone, type in the URL link "bit.ly/getquickthoughts" and press enter/go.

The opened page will lead you to an app that you are to install by clicking "Open". Once opened the app, you sign up by clicking the sign-up icon at the base of the displayed page. The next pop-up message that comes up will be "Register" which will be clicked on. Read through the terms and conditions, once you find them agreeable, click on the agreed icon displayed on the screen and your account will immediately be activated.

Next to that page is a page that displays zero-dollar balance on the phone's screen, it contains information showing how much has been given to members of the platforms. Directly underneath this is the displayed information which states "Begin earning rewards". At this stage, you can begin to fill in your basic bio-data and other information, click save at the end of the process to retain the information or Cancel to discard.

As a new user/member, there are a few things you can start benefitting from by taking part in simple surveys that can earn you a couple of rewards.

Setting Text Styles, Sizes & Brightness

Depending on your preference, there might be the need to change common features like text size, style, and screen brightness on the series 5 watch. This can be easily done by going to the settings section on the connected iPhone and adjusting the brightness level to your satisfaction. Though increasing the brightness level can demand more battery usage, however, they may be a need for it depending on the weather condition of the day.

Also, directly below it is the text size section which can also be used in modifying the text size by increasing or decreasing the scale feature.

Finger Gesture Useful for Time Telling

Another smart feature in watch series 5 is the gesture style of requesting time telling from the watch. To do this, you simply tap the screen with two fingers for a brief second and hear the watch tell the time. It's a really awesome feature when used.

Hide Private Information When on the "Always on Display" Mode

We would want certain information to stay hidden on your watch even when it is on "Always on Display" and your wrist is in the down position.

One of the nice features in the apple watch series-5 is the ability of users to prevent your watch screen from displaying certain information. For users who wish to protect personal or sensitive information from being displayed on their apple watch screen, by following the steps below using your connected phone.

1. You go to the "settings" icon on the phone and click on "brightness & text size". Underneath the feature "brightness" is the feature "always-on".
2. On clicking this it will lead to the page displaying the sub-feature "Hide sensitive complications". This should be activated by clicking it to make it come On.

What this does by implication is that whenever the watch is facing downwards when on your wrist, sensitive information such as calendar appointments, heart rate, mail messages, and the likes would be automatically hidden.

Setting Up Emergency SOS

The emergency SOS feature is a very important tool, especially when it is called upon to help in averting life-threatening situations. It allows you to be able to easily make urgent calls.

To activate it, you go to your Apple Watch app on your iPhone, you click on emergency SOS, then you enable automatic dialing, which is usually "off" by default so as to be able to call emergency services if you press and hold the side button for a few seconds.

You should also turn on the fall detection feature so that the apple watch can automatically dial the contacts of emergency services when you press and hold the side button.

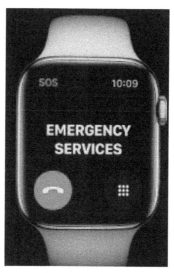

Note that before the watch proceeds with the command, it will give a brief notification confirming if you actually want to proceed with the dialed request. This is a good feature as it will help in avoiding cases of false emergency calls, especially when the command is mistakenly activated.

So, in summary, the emergency SOS service is a feature that helps you access emergency services faster, especially in critical situations where you can't do much with your body.

General Features and Settings of The Apple Watch Series 5

Basically, in exploring the watch's features and functions, you can perform simple basic operations to get familiar with the watch's functionalities like tapping on screens to activate for operation, tapping the side button, using the digital crown button to scroll and zoom displayed options, press and hold screen to move around so as to see the different available applications.

To explore selected applications, you can simply tap on the application and the selected or tapped application will be open for use. An example is the process that was followed when making the I-watch and iPhone synchronization in which the application "settings" was tapped to access its functions.

This same procedure is what is followed when using more frequently used applications like Mail apps, Contact book, Messages, Instagram, and WhatsApp.

Rearranging the Position of App Icons

It is not uncommon for certain users not to like where the displayed icons/apps are positioned, in such cases, you have the option of making changes to these displayed icons by first tapping on the icon/app you wish to be changed and subsequently dragging it to any part of the watch's screen. A similar process is also often carried out on a regular smart phone's display screen.

This can be achieved on the iPhone by simply going into "My watch application", and then select the icon "App Layout" after which you press and hold any of the desired displayed apps on the screen and repositioning it to a new location as or in replacement of a former one.

So, in summary, displayed applications on the apple watch series-5 can either be done from your watch or from the connected phone.

Text Size & Format

Apart from the general watch display settings and display customizations, there is also room for general settings such as phone's brightness and text size. These can be easily done from the watch's screen or from the iPhone's screen.

To adjust the brightness of the watch's screen, simply click on the icon "Settings", after which you scroll down to the "Brightness & Text-size" option. You can then click on any of the features to effect the required changes by making the adjustments for the display as required, especially things like brightness and contrast.

Similarly, the text size can also be changed depending on your preference, so as to make the text more legible and make it easy for your eyes.

Apart from the text size, another option also exists that is called "Bold Text", which is located under the "Text Size". It is a very impressive feature, especially when you want to get more readable information by looking at your watch because of the way it thickens or bolds the text format and text style. However, due to the fact that this feature is always switched off by default, if you are interested in activating it, you can easily click on it so as to activate it.

Sound & Haptics Settings

Additionally, you can adjust the watch's sound and haptics. This is where the projected sound from the watch can be modified to suit you, by making it louder or softer. There is also the "Mute" feature which can be used to mute the device.

Shortcuts to Silencing the Watch

In order to quickly access silencing features like Airplane mode, Mute, Do not disturb, & Pin your iPhone, you simply swipe up and scroll to the left until you see the connected Tab from where you can select what you want by simply tapping the feature on the displayed screen.

By tapping or activating the "Do Not Disturb" mode, this will prevent the getting or seeing of notifications on the apple watch.

To deactivate the mode, you will simply follow the process which was followed in activating it. Once it is deactivated, it will take some few moments under (one minute) before the network mode becomes fully active.

You can also turn off the sound of the watch by turning on the Silence mode, but this will still keep the haptic feature on. So, in order to turn off both sound and haptic, you will need to turn on the Do not disturb feature.

Finding iPhone With the Series-5 Watch

Another awesome feature of the apple watch series-5 is that it can be used to easily locate phones misplaced not too far away around the home, office, or environment.

To access this feature, you simply swipe your watch display screen up, after which swipe left, and below the silencing mode features is an icon with the image of the phone emitting radiation-like pattern. You click on it and immediately it is going to send a form of pinging message to the iPhone, which can be heard if the iPhone is within the vicinity, making it very easy to find misplaced iPhone. This can be done as many times as possible when trying to find a misplaced iPhone.

Checking Battery Status

From the menu's, just like the silencing mode that has a list of quick view features of the watch, you are also able to check the battery level by swiping across the same menu list to access the battery level icon at a glance.

In this same feature, there is a feature called the POWER RESERVE. This feature is useful in conserving the battery level of the watch when the watch's battery is low. On activating, the watch will be able to display the time, but other applications on the watch will not be available for use on the phone.

To access this mode faster, you can simply click on the watch's side button and select the power reserve mode option by swiping to the right. This simple tweak will significantly help you conserve battery life. Note that once this feature is activated, no feature on the watch will be in operation, even as little as the screen displaying when been tapped.

So, to have other applications back in use, you will need to restart the watch by pressing the side button which also serves as the power button.

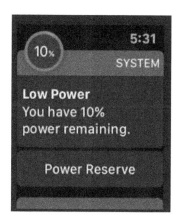

Customizing Watch Face

The Apple Watch Series 5 allows you to easily configure and design the appearance or display of the watch to creating a nice appearance to suit your personality.

Some of such display options include; utility, Modular, Simple, Motion, Color, Astronomy, Solar, Chronograph, Mickey, and X-large.

You can also decide to customize your screen display by changing it from the default display option.

To customize the face of your watch, you simply click on "new" from the last default customized display options. Once that is clicked, you are then prompted to select the type of watch face you want. In exploring available options, the digital crown can be used in selecting the selected watch face design.

To get started, simply press and hold the display screen to bring out some default display options which can be chosen from.

In customizing a watch's face display, the principle remains the same, for example, you can select the "Utility" design type. Once you select it, you then tap on customize. You can use the digital crown to check various customization options for the selected face type that can include desired clock numbers, background color selection, date format, and positions of features to be displayed.

Additionally, the bottom display section can include any selected content by you. And when you are satisfied with the display modifications, the home button at the side of the watch on the digital crown can be tapped and changes effected.

Notifications

The notification feature on the Apple Watch Series-5 screen displays in a unique style. And this is noticeable when a red dot is displayed on the top part of the watch's screen which means that you have an unread notification. To check these notifications, simply swipe down the screen to access and read through them.

At the same time, there are a number of actions that can be instantly carried out when the message is opened and read, you can decide to "Reply" or "Dismiss". For instance, to reply, you can tap on "Reply" which will open up preset responses like "Yes", "No", "Absolutely", Smiley, or using "Siri" to dictate voice messages into texts which will instantly transcribe the spoken word. If you find the transcribed words to be what you intend it to be, then you can simply tap on it to send.

The Apple Pay and Passbook

In setting up the passbook and apple pay on the apple watch series-5, you will have to use the connected iPhone, go to My watch and select Passbook & Apple play. You can decide to set up a credit card and add both credit and debit cards.

To access the Apple Pay when you are in the store, you simply double-tap the side of the power button on the smartwatch. Apple pay will be contacted for the selection of purchases in different stores.

To access the passbook on the smartwatch, you should go to the watch's home page, the swipe and search for the passbook application and open with just a tap. Here, you will be able to access the passbook application, through the smartwatch.

Using Apple Watch Series-5 To Access Benefits from Ebates Application

Another service on Apple Watch is known as Ebates. Ebates is simply an online service that allows you to benefit from cash backs on all of your online orders or purchases. The service has an app for iPhone users.

To get started, you will have to use the browser on the phone and type in the URL; bit.ly/appfindebates, the link is going to load a page that prompts you to register. It will then proceed to display a number of offers in the form of gift card bonuses for different online stores. You can register or join by using your email or Facebook profile.

Ebate works by giving users of the app the opportunity to get instant cash backs on purchases made online. For instance, users on the platform can get up to 15% cashback from over 150 different stores from which they have made purchases including Amazon and eBay. For example, in such situations, for every $100 worth of purchase made on any of the approved sites, the person can get an instant $15 as payback subject to their terms and conditions. Additionally, coupons are also available as added benefits.

Whenever a purchase is to be made, you will go to your selected online store to make purchases. Once through with the purchase or transaction your ebate account will be instantly credited with bonus offer as cashback.

And to get a bonus gift card, you will need to spend at least $25 from any of your regular online stores and become eligible to be rewarded instantly. This app simply helps iPhone and Apple Watch Series 5 users get the best out of online shopping.

Things to Know About Glances

To explore the available glances on the apple watch series-5 which includes Silence mode glance, Airplane mode, Do not disturb, and Sound settings you have to swipe on the screen of the watch. Also swiping to the left to view the next glance is the music settings feature which can be used to play, pause, select next or previous songs, as well as control levels of music.

The music available to be played can be from the watch itself or from the connected iPhone. The next glance that can be accessed is the heart rate, which can be used to monitor the condition of your heart condition by reading the pulse rate of the heart.

Furthermore, is the battery status view which also reveals the option for instant "Power Reserve" mode. The next view is the Activity App and subsequently, the events view which can be used as a sort of planer for future activities.

The next glance is the weather condition in your locality, which immediately after is the stock market section where stock activities can be monitored.

Next on the view menu list is the map in which you can use to get information about your locality, and also use it in getting weather information of any areas you want information especially when you want to make a trip to those areas.

The current world time and gate can also be viewed from the watch's screen by checking the menu list after Map.

Setting Alarms, Timers, Stop-Watch, & World Clock

The features of the apple watch series-5 also include using alarms, setting timers, stopwatch, and world clock in a way that is similar to the ones found on apple phones.

Alarm: To activate this for use, go to the alarm icon and tap to open. Once opened, you can choose to set a new alarm by tapping and holding the screen to open the menu options for the alarm in which you can set the alarm time, alarm tone, snooze options, notification title, repeat mode and save settings options as soon as selected details are set.

Timer Application: To activate this, you would have to go to the timer icon on the watch and open it with a simple tap. Once opened, the displayed options will be the timer that can be set to count down. Once the setting is done, you can exit the timer application to some other applications on the watch, this will not affect the set time on the timer application.

In using the timer, you have the option to set the timer to the home screen display on the watch mode. This can easily be done by making the display adjustments using the "customize" settings mode.

World Clock Feature: To access the world clock feature, simply go to the world clock application on the watch and tap to open.

Once the application is opened, you will see an array of default world time/clock like Cupertino & Network.

Stopwatch: The stopwatch functionality is another feature that can be accessed on the apple watch series-5. Once opened, the application contains a list of different display modes that you can choose from in line with your preference.

After choosing the selected display option, there is a start and stop sign that can be used to set the start and stop mode which are in green and red colors respectively.

Managing Messages on The Apple Watch Series-5

To get started using the message application on the apple watch series-5, you will need to open the message icon with a simple tap after locating it. Once opened, all record message histories & activities can be accessed. The opened message on the smartwatch will be automatically opened on the watch screen as well so that you can easily and quickly access the message for quick actions like a response if need be. Each message can be acted upon by opening with a simple tap. For instance, messages can be replied, deleted, or forwarded just like regular messages on the iPhone. The message feature on the apple watch series-5 also includes the ability to send emojis as responses that can be chosen by tapping the emoji option and selecting the choice to be used.

And just like the emoji option is used to respond, the regular text option is also available. This can be accessed by simply clicking the "reply" option.

In addition to the text and emoji options as responses, you also have the cool option of using "Siri" to send messages that would be transcribed into texts.

To send a new message, you simply need to go back or open to the main message page. After this, press and hold the screen as a pop-up message will display requesting if you wish to create a new message, after which a simple tap on the request icon will open up the area where text content is to be inputted. After typing the message content, you can easily send the message to the contact easily right above the text body option by selecting from your existing contacts or typing a new contact.

Managing Emails on The Apple Watch Series-5

Using the email application on the apple watch series-5 is very easy and user-friendly. Once opened, the email app displays your email content which at first are the messages in the inbox section.

To access received mail messages, you will need to open the message with a simple tap. Unfortunately, you cannot reply to such received email messages from the watch with a text, this can only be done from the connected phone. However, a unique feature that is exclusive to the apple watch series-5 under the email application is the hands-off instant email message response. If a user has an email opened on your connected apple smartwatch, then you can go to the connected iPhone. Here, at the bottom left corner of the lock screen display mode, you will swipe the screen up, and enter the password. After this, the screen will open directly to the received mail and open an email message on the connected smartwatch.

Additionally, you can also perform a number of operations in the email application on the Apple Watch like swiping left on the message to archive such emails, open emails with a simple tap on the selected email, press and hold to perform a number of operations on emails like when you want to flag an email as important, mark as read, as well as archive.

Making Calls on The Apple Watch Series-5

One of the coolest features of the apple watch series-5 is answering phone calls. For instance, when you have an incoming call, the displayed options will include the name of the caller (if it has been stored) and if not the phone number of the person will be displayed, options such as answer and reject will be presented with green and red icons on display. Also, on swiping up, you will be able to access further options such as send a message, answer on the iPhone.

If you wish to answer from iPhone, the call will be on hold and you will be able to answer on the iPhone.

There are further available icons or options if you choose to answer using the apple series-5 smartwatch, and these are; the volume option, voice/call record, and the call-end button.

Calendar and Reminder Features

Keeping of planned events or activities on the apple watch is very easy and efficient. To access this easy to use feature, you tap on the calendar icon which is displayed among the list of applications on the home screen display. Once opened, you can easily set and keep a list of planned activities, which can include the activities, time, date as well as other relevant info.

The calendar feature can also be easily added to the home screen for easy and quick access by you anytime.

To set this as part of the home background display feature, you will go to the home display background, hold and click on customize, after which choose the calendar option in whichever way you prefer it to be displayed and save. Once saved, you will be able to see planned activities at a glance on the watch display screen.

In addition to this, the reminder will always appear on the watch's notification bar, and when swiped down you can get updates or reminders on scheduled activities.

The Health and Fitness Tracker Feature

The health and fitness tracking fitness features of the apple watch series-5 is one of the many reasons people acquire this top-notch smartwatch.

To get the best out of this feature, you'll have to swipe up from the watch screen display page, swipe to the glance or view that has the Set Up the Activity App and click on it. Once opened, the displayed view will be that of three directional arrows appearing in three different colors with the displayed message underneath that states; "Activity, live a better day by achieving 3 daily fitness goals."

The Activities and three daily goals contain the following;

Stand: Stand for at least 1 minute of every hour of the day.

Move: Achieve your personal goal to have your calories burnt from your movement each day

Exercise: Accumulate up to 30 minutes of activity through brisk walks and other exercises.

At the end of these displayed options, the final notification will display the summarized previous messages, and you can then click on the Get Started icon to begin accessing the application fully.

The first page consists of a request form in which you will be expected to fill a bio-data form which includes your sex, age, weight, etc.

Once the information has been successfully filled, you can easily monitor the different health activities like different calorie burn goals such as moving and exercise.

Swiping further to the right, you will be able to view the data about certain activities done as calories burned, time spent, and target time.

The monitoring of these activities can also be easily done using the Apple Watch application on your connected phone as well.

To have it on display on the background clock display menu, then you can easily follow the customize procedure and have it fixed on the selected part of the watch face.

Workout App

The workout app allows you to easily manage individual workout sessions, some of which are available for display on the app like walking outdoors, running, outdoors, cycling outdoors, indoor walking, cycling indoor, and other workout activities. Depending on What feature is chosen, you can set the calorie target, time budget, and start.

Maps

The Apple Smart Watch offers a number of map features when connected to the apple map application. The digital map crown can be used to zoom in and out of the map. Additionally, by pressing and holding the screen in the application, you can search for nearby locations using the search icon. Here you will simply need to input the desired location in the search icon and view the displayed result. Also, you can also search and use the map application.

The Meaning of the Various Icons on The Apple Watch

Status icons and symbols usually appear at the top of the Apple Watch Screen. The following are the status icons and symbols along with what they signify or mean.

Status icons and symbols usually appear at the top of the Apple Watch Screen. The following are the status icons and symbols along with what they signify or mean.

1. The symbol ⚡signifies a low battery
2. The symbol ⚡shows the Apple Watch is charging.
3. ✈ signifies that the airplane mode is on. All wireless features will be turned off when the airplane mode is on.

4. ☾ shows the "Do Not Disturb" feature is turned on. Calls and alerts won't ring out or display any light except this setting is turned off.

5. The Theater Mode is signified by 🎭 when the feature is on. The screen remains dark until you tap the screen, turn the Digital Crown or press a button as the Silent Mode is on. This mode ensures the screen remains dark, even when the "Always On feature" is being used in the Apple Watch Series 5. By opening the Control Center and tapping the icon, the Theatre Mode can be turned off.

6. The icon 📶 appears in the control center when the Watch is connected to a Wi-Fi network rather than to your iPhone.

7. 📶 suggests a connection between a Cellular network and your Apple Watch with GPS + Cellular. The signal strength is indicated by the number of dots displayed.

8. 📵 this shows there is no connection between your Apple Watch and your iPhone. Ensure the Airplane Mode is turned off or move your devices close to each other as the case may be.

9. When the symbol ✕ displays, there is a lost connection between the Cellular Network and your Apple Watch with the GPS + Cellular.

10. 💧 is the "water drop icon" which shows the "Water Lock" feature is on. The screen won't respond when being tapped. The Digital Crown is turned to unlock the Apple Watch. This "water drop icon" can only on Apple Watch Series 2, 3, 4 and 5. They are all suitable for swimming and has water resistance.

54

11. When this ● shows, it means you have a notification. To read it, you need to swipe down on the face of the watch.

12. ● This is the audio output button. To switch the audio output between paired accessories like Bluetooth, tap the audio output.

13. ◤ This shows one of the apps on your Apple Watch made use of your location services.

14. 🔒 This shows your Watch is locked. Tap and input the passcode to unlock.

15. When you navigate a third-party app, this ➤ appears. The device may need a restart if the icon still displays after the navigation has ended.

16. The workout icon 🏃 appears when the "Workout app" is being used.

17. ● This icon represents the "Walkie-Talkie. You can connect with friends immediately by tapping to open the app.

18. The "Now Playing icon" ⫿ displays when an audio is playing.

19. ◑ shows when you are receiving directions in Maps.

20. ⋯ It means an active process is on or a wireless activity is ongoing

21. When the phone app icon ● shows, it means there is a phone call in progress.

Chapter Four

Using the Apple Watch Series 5 App Store

Apple Watch Series 5 comes preinstalled with watchOS 6 which comes with a dedicated App Store that makes it easy to find, download and install apps right from your wrist. With this app, the need to always use your iPhone to find apps for use on your Apple Watch will be reduced. As expected, the app store on the Apple Watch is not nearly as robust as the iPhone's Watch App Store. It, however, makes installing apps a little easier and can be used effectively, albeit with a bit of patience.

Searching for Apps on the App Store on Apple Watch

If you already know how to search for apps on the iPhone, then searching, for apps on the Apple Watch will be a breeze. To do that, follow these simple steps:

1. Go to your Apple Watch's Home screen by pressing the Digital Crown
2. Open the App Store by tapping on it or you can ask Siri to launch the app

3. Tap on Search to initiate the process for searching for apps
4. Select a method to use from the dropdown available. You can choose to either use Dictation or Scribble

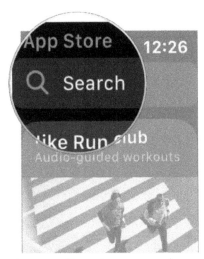

5. Speak if you choose dictation or write out the name of the app if you choose scribble to find the app you want

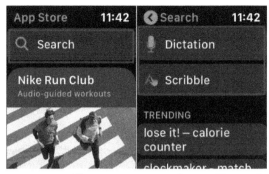

6. Tap Done to confirm your search or Cancel to discard your search

If the app you are searching for does not appear from your search on the Apple Watch Series 5, it may be because the app is not supported on the Apple Watch, so you can opt instead to look for the App on the App Store on your iPhone.

Learn to Download Apps from the App Store on the Apple Watch

Use the method described above for searching for apps on the App Store on the Apple Watch to confirm the app you want to download

1. Tap on the app you have chosen to download
2. Tap Get for free apps or the Price for paid apps
3. Tap Enter your password if prompted to do so
4. Select your preferred method of entering your password by tapping either scribble or your iPhone keyboard.
5. Enter your password
6. Tap Done on your Apple Watch or return on your iPhone

Your download will begin immediately onto the Apple Watch and iPhone.

Checking for Updates in the App Store on the Apple Watch

1. Go to the Home screen on your Apple Watch by pressing the Digital Crown
2. Open the App Store by tapping on it
3. Use your finger or Digital Crown and begin scrolling down to the bottom
4. Next, tap on Account when you find it

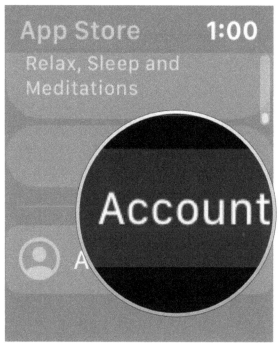

5. Then tap on Updates

When you do that, apps that require updates will show up so that you can decide to update all of them at the same time or select the ones you want to download one at a time.

Viewing Your Purchased Apps in The App Store on Apple Watch

1. Go to the Home screen on your Apple Watch by pressing the Digital Crown
2. Open the App Store by tapping on it
3. Use your finger or Digital Crown and begin scrolling down to the bottom
4. Next, tap on Account when you find it
5. Then tap on Purchases

Viewing App Ratings and Reviews on the App Store on Apple Watch

1. Go to the Home screen on your Apple Watch by pressing the Digital Crown
2. Open the App Store by tapping on it
3. Tap on the app you are interested in seeing their ratings and reviews
4. Scroll down to locate and tap Ratings & Reviews
5. To see more details, tap on "Read More"

Chapter Five

How to Create a Back-up of your Apple Watch

Backing your Apple Watch up Automatically

The backing up of the Apple Watch data is more about syncing that information to the database on your iPhone. Apple tends to ensure that most of its devices, including the Apple Watch Series 5 offer automatic backup services nowadays. The Apple Watch syncs your essential data by continuously syncing your data to your iPhone, which effectively ensures that you do not have to do your syncing manually.

The syncing process starts from when you successfully connect your Watch to your iPhone via Bluetooth or Wi-Fi by automatically syncing your Watch settings, recent Workout, Health, Activity, and app data. Any data related to health are treated as confidential and is only stored on your iCloud or iPhone as encrypted data. As a matter of fact, health-related data do not get stored at all if your version of iTunes is unencrypted, so it is always important to ensure that your backup is done via iCloud or iTunes backup that is encrypted. Certain third-party apps also provide some form of backup services.

Generally, Apple tries to ensure that things that pose security threats are not synced and that includes Bluetooth pairings, Apple Pay details, Apple Watch Passcode and any other detail considered personal by Apple.

Apple, however, considers the following suitable for syncing.

- Apple Watch Home screen layout
- Music-related settings, including playlists, albums, and singles
- General watch settings like brightness, sound, haptic and other system settings
- Current face settings, customization, and ordering
- App-specific data and settings for built-in apps like units, Maps, distance and third-party settings for apps like weather, mail, stock, Calendar.
- Data entered by users and notification settings
- Settings for Siri Voice's controls
- Syncing of photo album. To see what albums are syncing, from the Apple Watch app, tap the My Watch tab, then tap Photos > Synced Album.
- Dock settings, order, Watch pattern of usage, and available apps
- Time Zone
- Health and Workout data, including things like fitness info, workout progress, history, and Activity calibration data from your Apple Watch

Whatever data you sync between your Watch and iPhone stays locally on your iPhone, after which some of that data gets synced to iCloud. Depending on what option you decide to employ in your data backup, your health data will most likely get stored in iCloud and the others may get saved to iTunes when backing up your iPhone.

The importance of backing up your data on iCloud is that with your Apple ID you are able to restore your Apple Watch with very minimal data loss.

Backing up your Apple Watch Manually

What happens when you want to take matters into your own hands and back up your data manually to be sure everything is going on as it should? Well, the Apple Watch app doesn't have a button for backup that you can tap to initiate the process since the whole process has been designed to work automatically, however, if you are upgrading from a Series 3 or Series 4 and want to migrate to the Series 5 but want to be doubly sure that every information or data has been synced, you can do that by un-pairing your Apple Watch from your iPhone when they are still connected forcing it to trigger another sync with your iPhone.

So, if you are switching from one iPhone model to another, you start by unpairing your Apple Watch from your old smartphone, disabling your Activation Lock, and making a backup of your old iPhone.

The best time to undertake this process is when either your new Apple Watch or your new Apple phone is already available since the Apple Watch is designed to work when connected to any iPhone.

Restoring your Apple Watch from a Backup

Backing up your iPhone is only useful if you know how to restore that backup data to a new watch or on a new iPhone.

Follow the steps below to do that:

1. Start by pairing the Apple Watch with the iPhone using the instruction in the first chapter of this guide
2. Next, tap Restore from Backup button

3. Select the relevant backup

4. Accept the terms and conditions and continue

5. Enter your Apple ID to set up Activation Lock and Find My iPhone

6. Confirm your understanding of the Shared Settings implications for iPhone and Apple Watch by tapping OK
7. Next, tap on Create a Passcode to create a passcode for the Apple Watch or tap Add a Long Passcode to add a passcode longer than four digits or select Don't Add Passcode if you prefer not to have a passcode on your Apple Watch (Not recommended)

8. If putting a passcode, tap to create a four-digit passcode
9. Enter your passcode once more to confirm.

10. If you have an Apple Watch Series 5 with an LTE service that has not been set up yet or you had your plan canceled, you may be prompted to Set Up Cellular on your Apple Watch.

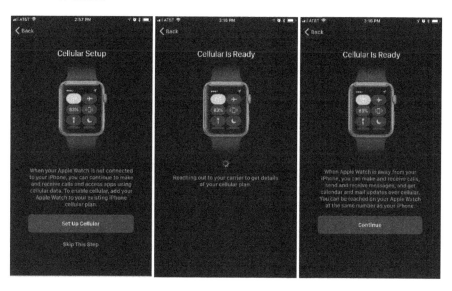

11. Tap Continue to confirm your understanding of Emergency SOS

12. You can also decide to set up Apple Pay if you do not want to be setting it up later. Setting up Apple Pay may require you to enter the entire number of your card or just the security code, depending on the type of card you're adding

The process for restoring your Apple Watch from your previous backup will now begin.

The restoration process can sometimes take a while, so Apple will present you with certain basic navigation tips called the Apple Watch Basics while this is going on.

Chapter Six

Suggested Apple Watch Apps for Your Series 5

The Apple Watch stands out among other brands of watches in terms of apps. A lot of apps can be found in the Apple Watch Store. Apps can easily be gotten directly from your Apple Watch with the launching of the on-watch App Store through the watchOS 6 updates.

Just in case you need a quick start or idea on which apps would give you the best performance, here are some of the recommended apps which cover a wide range of categories out of the hundreds of apps you can get from the Apple Watch Store. With the new Apple Watch Series 5, you will find them very delighting and useful when downloaded.

Suggested Workout App

One of the most common uses you can use the Apple Watch for is fitness tracking. Strava is tipped as the best workout app on the

Apple Store that has fully adopted GPS tracked running and cycling on Apple Watch. It has a pedometer that functions to provide you with information about your walks and runs. Strava also helps in monitoring your heart rate. It also provides audio feedback for when you begin or end an activity which many cyclists and runners find very useful. It works independently of an iPhone, so there is no need to work out with your iPhone.

Suggested Weather App

If you are looking for a decent weather app, the Carrot Weather app is a paid app worth spending on. It is an excellent weather app that presents an awesome Apple Watch App interface. It does not include intrusive ads, notifications or Information-heavy designs, that are inherent in some weather apps. The app has an "AI" feature that enables communication between the app and you. It is loaded with information and snarks. You can go to the app's settings to select any of the four humor levels depending on how you want the quirky robotic voice to communicate with you. The app which is unique for being straightforward, displays the current weather conditions, including hourly and weekly forecasts.

The hourly weather forecast is displayed using a scatter plot graph, with the temperature and weather conditions being represented with icons. The app displays hourly precipitation estimates using a bar graph. You can tap on the time to get information like humidity, wind, UV index and how the temperature feels like at the time. The daily section which is relatively smaller and displayed at the bottom of the screen has the weather and the day's high and low being represented by an icon. To get more information, you can tap on a day to expand the section. You can be notified if there are any extreme weather alerts from the section located at the top left-hand corner. Another fun added to the use of this app is the mini-game that tasks users to find locations on a map.

Recommended Sports Scores App

With the ESPN app installed on your Apple Watch, you can be sure to be updated on the scores of the team you support in virtually any sport. You can get breaking news alerts and competitions that keep you informed at a glance. Sports fans would find this useful as a way of tracking the progress of your favorite teams since you can now get information about live games being played in a formal and simple setting.

Suggested Gym App

The Carrot Fit is an awesome app that has the Malevolent Carrot AI that guides you through your paces with gym programs like "Celebrity Face Punches" and "Dragon dating Dances. When you start your workout, your Apple Watch gives you a heads-up display to let you know what exercise you need to be doing. You can pause things at will depending on how far your body can carry you through the exercise.

Suggested To-Do List App

The "Things 3" app is arguably the best bet you can get if you are considering having a to-do manager Apple Watch App. It helps you to focus properly on your current tasks. This can be displayed as a list and when the task is completed, it is ticked off and added to the list of completed tasks.

Recommended Note App

The Cheatsheet is a useful app that can help you make a tiny list of quick notes on your Apple Watch. The Cheatsheet is an app for both the iPhone and Watch. It is a good tool that serves as a reminder, especially to people who easily forget important things like a password, a new phone number, bank account number, etc. You can view your cheats on the Apple Watch 5 Series. They can also be added through dictation. There are specific icons that depict each item, thereby making it easier to identify.

Recommended App for Well Being

The "Streaks" is a good app that helps you form good habits. It is an Apple Watch app that is very flexible. You can define about 6 habits on your iOS device interface. You can choose your tasks to be either a one-off or timed task, with each task assigned to any specific day. Alternatively, you can choose to complete them in a particular predefined number of times as either weekly or monthly.

Recommended App for Audio Recording

With the "Just Press Record" app, you can now make quick recordings by tapping the record button, capture some audio, stop the recording as well as sync your audio recordings to the cloud, with your Apple Watch. Its ease of use in voice recording makes it a good pick. You can also talk to your wrist and later get a text copy of all you have recorded synced to your iPhone. Thanks to the excellent transcription features of the app which is a remarkable feature of the app.

Recommended Calculator App

PCalc is a calculator app that has an excellent interface and built-in conversions. The app is very responsive. It has a strong converter for metric to imperial units in addition to the basic math functions. The Digital Crown can be used to adjust conversion values.

There are other wonderful apps you can explore with your Apple Watch that will give you a good experience. Some of them are swim.com, WorkOutDoors, ActivityTracker Pedometer, Pear, One drop, AutoSleep, Mint, Fantastical 2, Chirp for Twitter, Messenger and others.

Recommended Apple Watch Games

There are games designed specifically for Apple Watch that can be found in the Watch's App Store. The App Store, which has the same appearance as on the iPhone can be found by pressing the Digital Crown to navigate to the App screen. These games are simple as the watch has limited size, resolution and control options. However, there are wonderful games designed for the wrist-sized screen that will give you all the fun you seek in playing games. The following are some of the top best Apple Watch games.

Pocket Bandit

This game uses the digital crown. In this game, your role is to be a safecracker, unlocking the safe combinations by spinning the crown before the timer runs out. The haptic feedback notifies you when you are getting closer. The game which costs around $1 is a good game for passing time.

Runeblade

This is a free adventure game that requires you to hack and slash your way along a tiny adventure. You can improve your weapons and armor while leveling up and managing inventory. The game has many levels of fantasy action. The one-tap play makes combat and interaction very simple. Runeblade gives you something close to hardcore gaming.

Lifeline

The Lifeline game is a perfect example of a text-based adventure game that gives players a real-time experience. You are to play the role of an astronaut who is stranded. You will be involved in bits of conversation with few reply options that you can tap. This game is a plus for lovers of sci-fi action. This game costs about $2.

Elevate

Elevate is one of the best Educational game that helps in exercising your brain. It made it to the Apple shortlist of App of the year in 2018. It has several brain teasers created to test your comprehension skill, numerical skill and lots more. The app has a free trial period of 14 days, after which you would be required to subscribe to the premium plan. It costs $40 per year. Alternatively, you can opt for a $5 per month subscription.

Pong

Pong is a free game that involves you, using the Digital Crown to move your paddle to keep the ball in play. The watch is your opponent. This game is unique to Apple Watch as it is absent from the iPhone.

Komrad

This game which can also be played on the iPhone is also a good example of a text-based adventure game that works very well on an Apple Watch. It is also a good interactive fiction game that makes you interact with a Soviet AI from 1985. The fate of the world is decided by you as you respond to KOMRAD from your wrist. The game costs about $1.

Letterpad

For lovers of word games, this free game is a good choice. You will be provided with nine letters by the game and be required to find words that are related to the current topic given. It is a kind of brain teaser that requires you to rack your brain. The game allows you to work through more than 200 puzzles for free. But there are in-app purchases, which provide you with hints to scale through tough levels and advance further in the game.

Twisty Color

Another interesting game that puts the Digital Crown into use is the Twisty Color game. It is a simple and straightforward game in which you are required to collect as many balls as possible by spinning the Twister to align with the corresponding color on display. It is a fun and addictive game that does not require any complex concept. You can purchase the game at $1.

Trivia Crack

This game is similar to Trivial Pursuit. You would be asked a lot of questions from different categories. You would be required to answer them using multi-choice answers. With this free app, you can spin the wheel, read and answer questions directly on your wrist wherever you are at any time.

Lateres

Lateres is a nice game where you use the Digital Crown as a control to the paddle, for aiming at the perfect brick-breaking action. Lateres also work on your iPhone. It provides you with about 20 levels for $1.

Tiny Armies

This tactical game, which costs a dollar, is available on both your Apple Watch and iPhone. You can engage in epic battles that are simplified conveniently on your wrist. All you need to do is to swipe the screen to defeat the enemies, move around the lakes, and proceed through mountains and forests.

Chapter Seven

Best Apple Watch Charging Stands

The security and safety of your Apple Watch is something you don't want to take for granted, hence the need for you to ensure you get a good charging stand that would not only protect your Apple Watch but also give it some style and finesse. The charging stands, which enable you to charge your premium watch also function as decorative pieces.

Here are some top charging stands you can get, that suit your Apple Watch Series 5.

Elago Charging Stands

The Elago charging stands draw inspiration from Apple's original Macintosh. Elago charging stands come in a number of excellent designs and colors perfectly suited for Apple Watches. The stands are mostly compatible with the Apple Watch Nightstand mode. One unique feature of this brand is that it is made from high-quality silicone, which is flexible and scratch-resistant. They are also affordable as the prices start from as low as $13. A good example of the Elago charging stands is the Elago W3. The bottom and top panels are made of silicon, which helps to protect it against damage. Cable management is made easy with its cylindrical design. The W3 is best for in-car usage.

Belkin Valet Charging Stand

Belkin is a household name known for modern electronic gadgets. The Belkin Valet Charging Stand is one of the stands you can bank on. It comes with a magnetic charging module that is inbuilt and integrated into an elevated armrest. The armrest which has an excellent metallic chrome finish enables the watch to be viewed from an optimal angle when being charged. It has a band support attachment. This charging has a base with a four-foot-long tethered USB cable. This can be used to power the stand with the aid of a wall adapter.

Spigen S350

The Spigen S350 is made of durable TPU material and also comes with a trademarked Nanotac pad base. This adhesive silicone pad holds your Apple Watch Stand, firmly. This charging stand has an open dock design that ensures easy use with your Apple Watch's bundled magnetic charging puck. You can charge your Apple Watch with the case on as the watch is compatible with the Apple Watch Nightstand mode.

This compact and lightweight nightstand is one of the best Apple Watch Stand that is affordable across the board.

Olebr

This is a three-in-one charging dock that can be used not just for your Apple Watch but also for your iPhone and Airpods. The coupling of the dock is quite simple and easy with the neat arrangement of the entire Apple ecosystem. It comes with a patented silicone tray, which holds your Apple Watch firmly at 45 degrees. You can view time or alarm in the morning as it is compatible with the Apple nightstand mode. The three pebbles' unique design which enables you to place your iPhone horizontally is a special feature of the OLEBR.

Apple Watch Magnetic Charging Stand

This simple Apple Watch Charging Dock is produced by Apple, and it comes with a one-year warranty. This simple and easy-to-use charging dock allows you to charge your Apple Watch in a flat position or on its side. The magnetic charging module, when lifted from the center of the stand allows you to prop your Apple Watch against it and your Apple Watch will go into the Nightstand mode automatically. This allows you to use it as a bedside alarm. The stand is compatible with all models of the Apple Watch.

WORKS FOR
* 3.5 - 10.5 Inches Devices
* Apple Watch Series 4/3/2/1
  (38mm,42mm, 40mm, 44mm)
*Apple AirPods

4.0in

4.7in

5.8in

7.9in

10.5in

Chapter Eight

Ways to Improve Your Apple Series 5 Battery Life

For a smart device like the Apple Watch, the battery life is very important if you want to get the best out of your smartwatch. The Apple Watch is expected to last for a minimum of 18 hours, however, there have been complaints about how the battery drains rapidly. The longevity of your Apple Watch battery life is mainly dependent on the usage and several other factors. There are several tips and tricks you can adopt to improve the battery life of your Apple Watch Series 5.

Disable Nonessential Notifications

One very important way of getting the best from your battery is to disable notifications from your watch that you consider not really important. Receiving a lot of unnecessary and random notification drains your battery faster than you can imagine. Keep only important notifications enabled. Notifications from social media like Facebook can be disabled as well as other nonessential apps that are less useful. You should enable notification for only the apps you consider important. Follow these steps to get this done:

1. From your iPhone, open the Watch app
2. Select "Notifications"
3. Scroll to "Mirror iPhone Alerts" and turn off the alerts you don't want to mirror on your smartwatch.

When this is done, your Apple Watch will no longer mirror alerts from the specific apps on your iPhone.

Activate Reduce Motion

Animation consumes power, thereby drains the battery of your smartwatch rapidly. Extend the battery life of your Apple Watch by turning on the "Reduce motion" function. This can be done either on your Apple Watch or from your iPhone.

Using your iPhone:

1. Open Watch app from your iPhone
2. Select "General" by tapping on it.
3. Then select "Accessibility"
4. Tap "Reduce Motion" and then turn on the switch by swiping the button to the right.

Manually Stop Workouts After an Exercise Session

Your Apple Watch can continue to run at higher power more than necessary if it doesn't detect workout has ended for some time. To save your battery from being drained further by the app, you can end a workout session manually by swiping the screen to the right and tapping "End".

Turn on Power Saving Mode

Another way to save your battery is to consider enabling the "Workout Power Saving Mode". It is a sacrifice you should decide to make, to save your battery. The "Always-on Display" and the heart rate sensor would automatically be turned off during walking and running workouts.

To turn on the "Power Saving Mode" of your Apple Watch, follow these steps:

1. Open the Apple Watch app from your iPhone
2. Select Settings
3. Select Workout
4. Turn on the "Power Saving Mode" by tapping it

Opt for Greyscale Mode

Black theme consumes little battery of your Apple Watch, unlike the color pixels that consume more power. A sure way of improving your battery life is to keep the screen of your Apple Watch black. The use of the "Greyscale mode" ensures the OLED display of the smartwatch consumes less power by turning the entire display to gray. Follow these steps to turn on this feature:

1. Move to the settings app on your Apple watch
2. Select "Accessibility"
3. Turn on the switch for Greyscale.

Reduce the Transparency of Your Smartwatch

Reducing the transparency of your smartwatch does not only enhance your reading experience, but it also conserves your Apple Watch battery. To reduce the transparency from your Apple Watch, follow these steps:

1. Open the Settings app
2. Select "Accessibility", then
3. Turn on the switch for "Reduce Transparency"

Retry Pairing Your Apple Watch And iPhone

If your iPhone and Apple Watch aren't well paired, it could also be a factor that contributes to the draining of your battery faster. Un-pair your smartwatch, then, try re-pairing it as a new watch. This should solve any battery glitch that might have been as a result of poor pairing. Follow these steps to do this:

1. Open Watch app from your iPhone
2. On the "My Watch" tab, tap your smartwatch at the top of the screen.
3. Tap the little "I" at the right side of your watch information
4. Select "Unpair Apple Watch", then, confirm your choice.

The next thing to do is to have your Apple Watch paired again with your iPhone. Ensure you reboot your Apple Watch and iPhone before pairing to remove the caches.

Always Keep Your WatchOS Updated

Battery issues might be solved by simply doing an upgrade of your Apple Watch Software. You can keep tabs on the latest update available by:

1. Go to the "Watch app" from your iPhone
2. Select "General"
3. Tap "Software Update"

It would tell you if an update is available.

Alternatively, you can check if an update is available in your Apple Watch by:

1. Go to "settings"
2. Select "General"
3. Tap on "Software Update"

Apple builds upon previous versions to correct several problems faced by you. It is likely that updating your Apple Watch software to the new version would save your battery from being easily drained.

Chapter Nine

Using Social Media on Your Apple Watch

How to Use Facebook On Apple Watch

You can browse Facebook easily on your wrist without your iPhone. Apple has embedded WebKit into the Apple Watch's operating system with the WatchOS 5 update. With the absence of a Safari browser on the Apple Watch, the WebKit engine allows a full web page to be opened when a link in an email or text message is being tapped. There are limits to what you can do on these web pages unlike on your iPhone, where you can watch YouTube videos. Here are some processes to scale through in order to launch Facebook on your Apple Watch screen.

1.   Send an email message to yourself. Include https://www.facebook.com in the body of the email. Ensure the email account is the same as the one you have set up for the mail program on your iPhone. This will enable you to read the email message on your smartwatch

2. From your smartwatch, launch the Mail app and go to the inbox of the mail client where the email was addressed to

3. After opening the inbox, swipe down on the screen to download new messages. The email will appear on your watch

4. Tap on the Facebook link after opening the message

5. After Facebook finishes loading, enter your login details to access your Facebook account.

Sending a text message will also work, but, with an email message, you can easily flag the email message containing the Facebook link for easy future reference. While the message is on screen, simply hold your finger down on the Apple Watch display. Tap "Flag". The email message will appear in the Flagged inbox. You can easily refer to this later on.

How to Use Facebook Messenger On Your Apple Watch

You can opt for a Facebook messenger on your Apple Watch and enjoy chatting with friends. Follow these steps to get that started on your Series 5 Apple Watch.

1. Start the "Watch app" from your iPhone

2. Check if Messenger is already installed by tapping "My Watch" button at the bottom of the screen

3. At the "Installed on Apple Watch" section, select "the Messenger" if it is listed, to confirm if the "Show App on Apple Watch" option is turned on

4. To add the app to your Apple Watch, type "Messenger" into the search box located at the bottom of the screen.

5. You should see the Messenger app close to the top. Tap "Get" or the button with the cloud to get the app downloaded to your Apple Watch

How to Use WhatsApp Messenger On Apple Watch

WhatsApp which is one of the foremost used social media platforms is, unfortunately, not available in the Apple Watch Store. WhatsApp can be used on your Apple Watch with limited features that only allow you to receive and reply messages in simple formats. To use WhatsApp on your Apple Watch Series 5, follow these steps.

1. Get WhatsApp installed on your iPhone
2. From the WhatsApp on your iPhone, go to "Settings"
3. Select "Notification"
4. Select "WhatsApp Messenger"
5. After that, go to the "Allow Notifications and Show in Notification Center" option and turn on
6. From your iPhone, open the "Watch app".

7. Open "Notifications" in the "Watch app". All supported apps would be displayed.
8. Scroll down to find the "WhatsApp Messenger App"
9. Activate the notification button.

Having followed these steps, you should start receiving all your WhatsApp notifications on your Apple Watch Series 5. You should be able to read and reply to all messages from your contacts on your Apple Watch main screen.

How to Use Viber app on the Apple Watch

The Apple Watch also allows you to use the popular mobile messaging app Viber on its platform. Although as with WhatsApp the functions available for use tend to be somewhat limited, even then it is possible to use the app in an easy and efficient manner.

The app will enable you to read and respond to messages directly from your watch. You can even use it to send exclusively created stickers for the Apple Watch, all done without you having to pull out your iPhone from your pocket.

Viber provides the most secured instant messaging and calling apps that you can use across many Apple devices. It comes with an endless list of features that is sure to create a great Viber user experience that can even be better than some regular messaging platforms.

Just like other Apple Watch apps, Viber allows you to respond to incoming messages with canned responses, stickers from Viber and dictation. With the Viber for Apple Watch, you can do the following:

- Read messages and respond to them
- Follow your Viber conversations.
- Track your Viber activities and notifications, simply by glancing
- Make your responses more engaging with an exclusive Sticker Pack for Apple Watch

Setting Up Viber for Apple Watch

Installing Viber on the Apple Watch is easy. To add the Viber app on your Apple Watch, you will need to use your connected iPhone to be able to access Viber on the Apple Watch.

1. Find and open the Apple Watch App on your iPhone and tap it to open
2. Tap on the App Store icon at the bottom of the screen
3. Type Viber in the search bar to search for it
4. Click on the search button at the bottom to begin the search
5. Tap on the Get button to start the downloading process
6. The Viber app will show up on the Apple Watch as soon the downloading process is complete

Transferring an Existing Viber on the iPhone to the Apple Watch

If you already have Viber on your iPhone, you can simply tap on the Apple Watch app to open it. You can then scroll down until you find the Viber app

1. Tap it and tap on the slider to Show App on Apple Watch

2. The Viber app should now be installed on the Apple Watch

Opening Viber Messages on Apple Watch

1. Tap the Viber app on your Apple Watch home screen to open it
2. Select the chat within your chat list you would like to see the content

Alternatively;

1. Tap on Reply 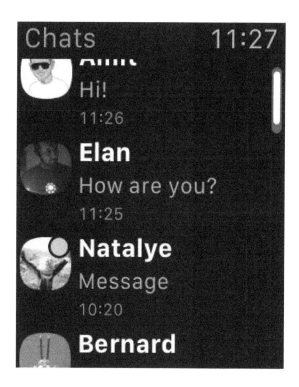 from the notification from Viber with the button that looks like an arrow or a plane

Responding to a Viber Message with a Sticker

1. Tap the Sticker icon on the message screen  Select the Sticker from the special Apple Watch's Sticker Pack you wish to send

Respond with Predefined Text to a Viber message

1. On the message screen, tap the reply icon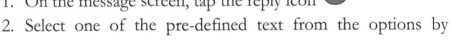
2. Select one of the pre-defined text from the options by scrolling through the them

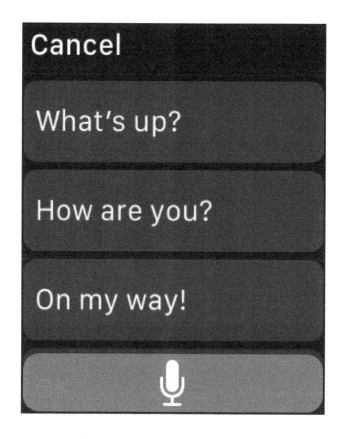

Respond with Siri to a Viber message

1. On the message screen, tap the reply icon 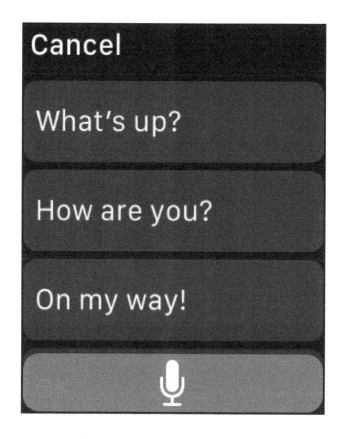 select the microphone icon from the options to use Siri

2. Start speaking with a clear tone at a distance not too far from the Apple Watch to begin the recording

3. Select Done when the recording is complete and want to send the message

Chapter Ten

Advanced Tips and Tricks on The Apple Watch Series 5

As with most smart devices, glitches are bound to occur which affects the proper functioning of your Apple watch. This can sometimes be caused by an app or your Apple Watch itself. However, you need not worry much. A simple restart and reset of your Apple Watch should get it back on track. Follow these steps to Turn off and Reboot Apple Watch.

Digital Crown/
Home button

Side button

1. Press and hold down the side button on your Apple Watch. A three horizontal slider would display.
2. Ensure your Apple Watch is not connected to its charger, to enable the use of the slider.
3. Move the "Power Off" toggle to the right.
4. Turn it back on by pressing and holding the side button until the Apple logo appears.

How to Force Restart Apple Watch

1. Press and hold both the Digital Crown and the Side Button of your watch together

2. Hold them until the Apple logo appears and the screen goes dark

Using the Workout App on Apple Watch Series 5

The workout App is quite different from the Activity app. The Workout app gives you real-time information such as calories burned, elapsed time, speed, distance and pace for your walks, jogs, cycling, etc. Activity App, on the other hand, shows you mainly your progress over the past day.

The Apple Watch would turn on specific sensors like the heart rate monitor, GPS, gyroscope, and accelerometer when you choose the type of workout you would like to embark on. A detailed summary of your exercise would be provided. Goals can also be set by you while you chart your progress and earn awards. Follow these steps to use the Workout app on your Apple Watch:

1. Go to the Home Screen by pressing the Digital Crown Button
2. Select the "Workout app" by tapping it. Alternatively, raise your wrist and say "Hey, Siri Workout."
3. Options for different types of indoor and outdoor exercises would be displayed.
4. Select a workout by swiping up or down or twist the Digital Crown button forward or backward to pick your choice.
5. After selecting the activity you like, tap it to be taken to the goals screen where you can pick a goal

6. Choose one option to set a goal. You can also customize each option to your goals.
7. Press "+" or "–" to increase or reduce the number respectively. If your goal is time-based, you can select the number of minutes that seems convenient to you.
8. Press "Start" close to the bottom of the screen to start your workout.
9. You would receive progress updates that can serve as a source of motivation for you during your workout.
10. To pause or end your workout, press firmly on your watch screen. You can also return to the Home screen by pressing the Digital Crown button.
11. To see a summary of your workout, swipe through the Workout screen

Having reviewed the goals you have achieved, you can decide to repeat an exercise with the same goals set. You can also choose to increase or decrease the goals.

How to Get Directions on Your Apple Watch Series 5

Apple Watch uses its built-in Map app to get directions from your current location to any destination you choose. It gives you turn-by-turn navigational instructions, which guide you through to your destination. Nearby businesses can also be found by asking "Siri".

Follow these steps to use the Maps App on your Apple Watch.

1. Go to your Home Screen by pressing the Digital Crown Button
2. Select the Maps app.

3. Alternatively, raise your wrist and say "Hey, Siri, Maps". As soon as the app opens, an overhead map of your current location is displayed on your Apple Watch screen.

4. Press and hold the Watch screen to activate Siri and then mention the address or business name you want to find.

5. After seeing selecting the location you want directions for, tap "Done" at the top right of the screen.

6. Select "Start" to map your route. You should get to your desired destination if you follow the instructions provided by the Maps app

How to Add Friends to your Apple Activity

To add friends to your Apple Watch's Activity app, your friends have to also have the Apple Watch. Follow these simple steps to add your friends.

1. Using your iPhone, launch the "Activity App"

2. Tap "Sharing" located at the bottom-right corner of the screen

3. Tap on the "Get Started" button which is in the middle of the "Sharing" page.

4. At the top-right corner of the screen, tap the "+" button.

5. Select a contact by scrolling down to find the contact of the friend you want to add or search the friend by typing the contact's name in the "To" text field.

6. After selecting a contact, tap the "send" button at the upper-right corner of the screen. An invitation would be sent to your friend to link up in your Apple Watch's Activity app.

7. Once your friend accepts your invitation, you can view their progress in the Activity app

How to View the Progress of Your Friends on Your Apple Watch

1. Start the Apple Watch's Activity app.
2. Press the "Lock" button to open the "Apps" screen and tap all apps where necessary.
3. Tap on the "Activity app" icon.
4. Scroll to the Sharing" page. A list of friends you're sharing your Activity progress with will open.
5. Tap the name of the friend you want to view Activity progress.
6. The page will load your friend's Activity progress for the day for you to view.
7. If you feel like sending your friend a message, scroll down to the bottom of your page, tap "Send Message" and choose a message to send

How to Request an Uber From Your Apple Watch

You can request an Uber ride from your current location with just your Apple Watch. However, you can only request a ride from your current location using your Apple Watch, and then communicate your destination to the driver when he arrives. Ensure you have Uber app installed on your Apple Watch, then follow these steps below:

1. Press your Apple Watch's button, or raise your wrist to wake up your Apple Watch
2. Press the Power button. A list of currently used apps would display.
3. Press the Power button once to close any notification, if you have any. Then press the Power button again to open the app list
4. Select "All Apps"
5. Tap the "Uber app" icon to open Uber. If you see a message asking you to sign in or register using the Uber app on your iPhone to begin using Uber for your Apple Watch, simply open Uber on your iPhone. Wait for the message to disappear before proceeding
6. Wait for Uber to ascertain your location. Proceed once a time estimate appears on-screen. Note that you can only use your current location
7. Select "Request". This will place a request for a ride from the nearest Uber car that matches your last ride's vehicle category
8. In the middle of the screen, you will see an estimate of the time it would take the Uber driver to arrive

How to Eject Water from Your Apple Watch When Wet

You can go swimming with your Apple Watch Series 5 as it comes with a water resistance feature. Also, our frequent daily usage of the Apple Watch while carrying out other activities can get water inside the Apple Watch's speaker. Caution must be taken to prevent the Apple Watch from being exposed to soaps, lotions, perfumes and any other chemical substances that can negatively affect the water seal and acoustic membranes. If your Apple Watch gets wet at any point in time, follow these steps that will guide you on the easy and unique way to eject water from your Apple Watch Series 5.

1. Swipe up from the bottom of the screen of the Apple Watch to open the Control Center
2. Scroll down and look for the "Ejection" icon that looks like a water drop.
3. Tap on the "Water Drop" icon
4. You would be prompted to "Turn Digital Crown to unlock and eject water"
5. As you turn the Digital Crown, the Apple Watch screen is unlocked. The blue dots appear with sounds, prompting that it is pushing out all the water

Using the Apple Watch Breathe App

The Apple Watch Breathe app is a built-in app that pops up and tells you to take a deep breath and relax. Here is an easy guide on how to use the Apple Watch's Breathe app.

1. Go to "Honeycomb Menu"
2. Select the Breathe app from the groups of apps
3. Twist the Digital Crown to select your desired session length
4. Tap "Start"
5. Follow along with the graphics on the watch face and the haptic feedback on your wrist

You will get a reminder telling you to remain still, to inhale when the animation grows, and exhale when it shrinks. This will ensure you gain a good reading. The watch will vibrate a couple of times and then chime, showing a heart rate figure when you are done. Note that, some of your notifications will be muted during any session.

You can decide to adjust your reminders and also the nature of your sessions. To adjust the duration of your session, you can use the Digital Crown. To change to a different default option, simply follow these steps:

1. Go to the Apple Watch app on your iPhone
2. Select "My Watch" tab
3. Tap "Breathe"
4. Scroll down to "Use Previous Duration"

Also, you can decide to change the length of each breath if the default duration seems difficult for you to keep up with. Simply follow these steps:

1. Go to Apple Watch app
2. Go to "My Watch" tab
3. Go to "Breathe"

4. Select "Breathe Rate" and adjust it to the breaths per minute you want

To change the reminders your Apple Watch provides you with, follow these steps:

1. Go to the "My Watch" tab.
2. Go to the Breathe section and tap "Breathe Reminders".
3. Toggle any option to send them to the "Notification Center".

How to Combine Your Workouts

With the Apple Watch, you can chain your workouts together which saves you the time of having to rub your sweaty fingers around the screen to change from one workout to another. You can do this by simply swiping to the right and tap on the "+" button to add a new workout.

How to Use Apple Music on Your Apple Watch Series 5

1. Ensure you have the Apple Music app launched on your iPhone.
2. From your iPhone, start the "Watch app"
3. Scroll down to the "Music" tab
4. Tap on "Add Music". You would be taken to "Apple Music"
5. Choose to browse music by artists, albums, genres or playlists, and tap to add to playlist.
6. After that, sync music to Apple Watch. Ensure your Apple Watch is on its charging stand to enable transfer to

be done. Your Playlist would be "synced" after the update is completed.

How to Use Spotify On Apple Watch Series 5

Spotify app for Apple Watch is now available, although, features like "offline playback" and streaming over a cellular connection are not available. Follow these steps to get the basics of Spotify on your Apple Watch:

1. Open the "Watch app" from your iPhone
2. Go to the "App Store" tab, search for "Spotify" app
3. Install the app and then open it on your Apple Watch
4. Add and play music from Apple Watch Spotify app. You can add music to your library directly from the app itself
5. Tap on the "heart" shape to get the track added to your music library.
6. Recently played music across your Spotify account would be displayed when you swipe to the left.
7. To swap albums or playlists from here, simply scroll with your finger or use the Digital Crown

How to Play Music on Your Apple Watch Series 5 Without the iPhone

All you need to play music on your Apple Watch Series 5 without an iPhone is an active data or internet access and an Apple Music subscription. This will enable you to start streaming music on your Apple Watch Series 5. Alternatively, you can download the music to your Apple Watch Series 5 via the Apple Music app.

How to Connect Bluetooth Headphones to Your Apple Watch Series 5

To connect your headphones to your Apple Watch for the first time, follow these steps below:

1. Ensure you put your headphones in pairing mode
2. From your Apple Watch Series 5, go to the "Bluetooth Settings"
3. Tap the settings gear app icon on your Apple Watch and tap on the "Bluetooth option" to view the available devices
4. Tap on the headphones to select which you would like to pair. After doing this, the Apple Watch should be able to detect headphones and pair with them when they are ready at any given time, once they are turned on close to your Apple Watch. However, if music pumps out of your iPhone, press and hold on your Watch screen and select "Playback" to send it to your headphones.

How to Use Your Apple Watch Series 5 To Unlock Your Mac

Your Apple Watch can unlock your Mac easily without entering a password. The authentication comes from both the Apple Watch's passcode and the heart rate monitor detecting your presence. This ensures a secure authentication process. Here are the simple steps to explore this feature.

1. Set-up Auto Unlock. To do this, ensure you download macOS High Sierra on your Mac and enable the "two-factor authentication" on your Apple ID.

2. To confirm if your Mac supports Auto unlock, press down the "Option" key and click to select the "Apple logo", then, select "System Information". After that, tap on the "Wi-Fi" menu in the sidebar, then look for "Auto Unlock: Supported (or not)".

3. You will have access to your Mac computers when wearing your Apple Watch close by as long as you are set up with "Auto Unlock".

4. When you are ready to access your Mac without typing a password, "Wake Up" the Mac. However, you'll have to enter the password on the Mac the first time you log in after turning on, restarting or logging out of the Mac. Subsequent logins would be possible without typing in your password

Marc's MacBook Pro
Unlocked by this
Apple Watch

Setting Up Siri on Your Apple Watch

Siri is just like the assistant you have inside your iPhone. Siri can receive requests from you with your Apple Watch. It can also assist you in sending messages, making calls and getting directions.

Ensure your device is connected to the internet to enable Siri to fetch information, then, follow these steps:

1. From your Apple Watch, go to "Settings".
2. Select "General", then, "Siri"
3. Toggle the "Hey Siri"
4. Then, enable "Raise to Speak"

To control how you want Siri to speak back to you, scroll down to "Voice Feedback" in the "Settings" section. You can set Siri to respond all the time, respond only when you have headphones in or be controlled by the silent mode. Siri's Voice Feedback, when turned on, will make the volume match the volume that is within the "Alerts" tab of the Sounds and Haptics section in your Apple Watch. You can adjust the volume to your selected choice.

How to Change the Voice Of SIRI

1. From your iPhone, go to "Siri"
2. Search for "Siri Voice" and select one. It would be updated the next time the Apple Watch syncs back to your iPhone

Activating SIRI

After setting up Siri on your Apple Watch, there are two simple options of getting to ask Siri a question.

Raise Your Wrist

1. With your Apple Watch Series 5, to get the voice assistant's listening indicator to pop up, simply raise your wrist. This would make your Apple Watch wake up.
2. Then hold it close to your mouth and speak to Siri to respond to your query

Push the Digital Crown

Alternatively, to wake up Siri, simply press down the Digital Crown for the listening indicator to pop up. Then speak to Siri to get it to respond to your query

Deleting Native Apps

You can delete stock apps from your home screen. To delete any native apps, Press and hold down the icon of the app you wish to delete on the Home Screen, then select "Delete App".

Take Screenshot of Your Apple Watch

To take shots of the screen of your Apple Watch, quickly and simultaneously press down both the side button and the Digital Crown.

Increase Your Watch's On-Screen Text

To make the text on your screen bigger, go-to accessibility settings. Select "Brightness and Text Size" and change to your selected choice.

Conclusion

Although considered pricey the Apple Watch Series 5 continues to retain Apple's dominance of the smartwatch market share and it is not hard to see why. The series 5 builds on the successes of the previous Series but takes it the now improved larger screen design by including a small but important change that allows the screen to stay on all the time as a normal watch would.

Before that major update, previous users of the Apple watch had to either tap the watch's face or perform an elaborate rotation of the wrist when trying to get the screen to light up, now you can see what time it is by a simple glance from any angle and at any time.

As we have come to expect from Apple, the Series 5 is a top-notch technological work of art from one of the foremost technological companies in the world. If you are yet to try it out, I think you should because you will find it to be one of the most comfortable timepieces you could ever have the pleasure of strapping to your wrist. Not only that, the watch is sturdy and simple and as this guide has shown, it is simple to install and use. The wrist bands can easily be removed with a few simple lug manipulations.

The watch is also made from premium materials that you can be sure that you will not suffer from skin irritation and any other possible challenges.

www.ingramcontent.com/pod-product-compliance
Lightning Source LLC
Chambersburg PA
CBHW051057050326
40690CB00006B/752